Al Capone

A Biography of Chi~~~~'

Legendary Mafia

Part 1 of the US Gangster Se

Gary Nites

Table of Contents

Introduction

Al Capone had several nicknames, some he hated and some he really liked. As a reader of his biography, you will discover that these names also represented milestones in his life.

Christened with the Italian name Alphonse, Capone chose to be called "Al", his American name, to signify his citizenship and the beginning of his pursuit of the American dream. After a brawl in a bar, his face was wounded by a knife and he was called, "Scarface."

When he was a lowly bouncer and enforcer, he was called the "Big Fellow," for his massive bulk and threatening reputation. His friends called him "Snorky" for his penchant for style and lavish lifestyle. When he assumed control of his organization, he was simply called "Boss."

Finally and at the height of his power, he was called capo de tutti capi, not only the boss but the "boss of all bosses." He never truly assumed that title but everyone knew that he was the most powerful among all other families in Chicago.

This biography will tell you the people, places, events and also the bribes, crimes and hits in between those nicknames. Trace Capone's beginnings from the slums of New York where his family disembarked from one of the many ships carrying thousands of immigrants.

Walk with Capone on his path to ascension from a lowly bartender to becoming the lord of all Chicago. Find out how he was finally caught, in the most anticlimactic of events and discover his descent from his pedestal, to his later years, death and his legacy.

Introduction

Al Capone had several nicknames, some he hated and some he really liked. As a reader of his biography, you will discover that these names also represented milestones in his life.

Christened with the Italian name Alphonse, Capone chose to be called "Al", his American name, to signify his citizenship and the beginning of his pursuit of the American dream. After a brawl in a bar, his face was wounded by a knife and he was called, "Scarface."

When he was a lowly bouncer and enforcer, he was called the "Big Fellow," for his massive bulk and threatening reputation. His friends called him "Snorky" for his penchant for style and lavish lifestyle. When he assumed control of his organization, he was simply called "Boss."

Finally and at the height of his power, he was called capo de tutti capi, not only the boss but the "boss of all bosses." He never truly assumed that title but everyone knew that he was the most powerful among all other families in Chicago.

This biography will tell you the people, places, events and also the bribes, crimes and hits in between those nicknames. Trace Capone's beginnings from the slums of New York where his family disembarked from one of the many ships carrying thousands of immigrants.

Walk with Capone on his path to ascension from a lowly bartender to becoming the lord of all Chicago. Find out how he was finally caught, in the most anticlimactic of events and discover his descent from his pedestal, to his later years, death and his legacy.

Chapter 1 – The Mafia, the Hierarchy & Chicago

Telling Capone's story is impossible without telling the background of the Mafia, the hierarchies within the organization and Chicago itself. To tell Capone's story is to tell the story of the world and the underworld where he lives in, be it the Mafia and Chicago.

The word mafia is actually a general term that describes a type of syndicate that is involved in organized crime. It is known for its use for intimidation, protection racketeering and manipulation. As a mafia grows, it diversifies its activities to fraud, drug trafficking, loan sharking, gambling, smuggling, vote buying and murder.

It was in Sicily that the word mafia was first used for these groups. Although there are disputes to its origin, there are claims of Arabic roots. Regardless of the origin, the mafia is an international phenomenon that appears across time, space and groups. Mexicans use the term La Eme, Japanese calls groups yakuza, Russian label it as Bratva, the Chinese use a term that is literally translated into Three Harmonies Society or the Triad. Finally and most popular is the Sicilian and American mafia that call themselves, Cosa Nostra.

The American Mafia, of which Capone belongs, has many names. It was called the Italian Mafia, the Italian Mob or simply the Mob. When large groups of Italian immigrants populated the United States, they brought along criminals, shady individuals and other members of different mafias. Giuseppe Esposito and six other Sicilians are always labeled as the first mafia members to cross into America. They fled to New York after murdering eleven Sicilian upper class landowners and two politicians of a Sicilian province.

The potency and efficiency of the mafia is credited primarily to two principles. Its hierarchy and its rules called Omerta. The hierarchy provides a chain of command that provides enough independence for individual cells to conduct their specific roles and responsibilities and enough control to keep order in the ranks and respect for authority.

On the bottom are the associates. They are usually regarded as tools and not as true members yet. They can range from non-Italians who do menial tasks to corrupt officials who protect the clan. They can be burglars, lawyers, assassins, police and other personnel who are on the payroll.

Next is the picciotto or the "little man." They are the lowest ranking true members of the mafia. Their role is to enforce the laws of Omerta through and amongst its associates. Of somewhat equal position is the soldato or the "soldier." If the mafia is an army, they are the foot soldiers. Each sub unit of a large mafia can have from 10 to more than 30 soldatos.

Commanding the soldatos is a caporegime or capo. He acts as the intermediary between the either the underboss or the boss and the soldiers. Capos experience the first taste of social status, respect and influence in the hierarchy. Each capo and his team of soldatos operate independently; they have their individual criminal activities. For example a family may have a capo in charge of their gambling dens, another in drug smuggling, some capos also engage in completely legitimate businesses such as stores, construction and even restaurants. Each cell collects the revenues of their activities, takes a share and surrenders the rest of the collection to the underboss.

Third in command, ranking only below the underboss and the boss is the consigliere or the "counselor." This is a person that occupies a position of trust and expertise. He is usually relied on by the bosses to provide guidance on their activities, such as a lawyer for legal matters, accountant for financial dealings and other professions. He can represent the boss for meetings with other families and is expected to argue with the bosses to ensure that plans are perfected.

The capo bastone or the "club head" is the second in command to the entire family. Depending on the family, he can either be a powerful member or marginal figurehead acting only to assist the boss. However, most capo bastones are traditionally close relatives to the boss. They are the boss' sons, nephews or in-laws by virtue of marriage. Since the underboss is in charge of the day-to-day administration of the family, he usually becomes next in line to the boss position.

The capo bastone also occupies a very important role. Should the boss be incapacitated, such as imprisonment, sickness or any other reason that will prevent the boss from making decisions for the family, the capo bastone temporarily assumes the leadership of the family. He is also expected to mediate during internal disputes and can command his own caporegime and soldatos. The underboss is often made purview to almost all secrets of the family, making him one of the most powerful and at the same time most vulnerable for incrimination.

Finally, there is the boss, the capo crimine or the "crime boss." This is the Don and the head of the entire family. He has absolute power over every member of the mafia. He has the power to spare and take lives, making him feared and respected. He is ruthless in his decisions but can be merciful in his forgiveness. All profits are given to him and he dispenses them based on his will alone. Bosses can promote, demote and initiate potential members to the family.

Due to his position, a boss will rarely perform or order any criminal activity himself. He delegates this orders to either the underboss or the advisors so that there is deniability. Most trials fail because evidences cannot directly implicate a boss.

An unofficial position in the hierarchy used only by the media and law enforcement is the capo di tutti capi or the "boss of all bosses." This position is meant to describe the most powerful and most influential boss among all other heads of families. It is rarely used by a boss since it can only provoke other families and risk unwanted violence. In fact, when a boss declared himself a capo di tutti capi, he was murdered. Another position in the hierarchy is the capo di capi re, a title of respect for retired senior members of the family.

Omerta are the set of tenets that are prescribed by every family to its members. While hierarchy gives command, Omerta gives order. Its main principle is that it is a code of silence. When the mafia applied Omerta in their rules it translated into the avoidance of interference, absolute privacy and secrecy and an opportunity for vengeance.

Omerta prevents the meddling of one sub unit of the family to another sub unit and the interference of an entire family's activities to another. This means, there a boundaries and territories that must be acknowledged and respected. Often, when crossing from one territory to another, a member must seek permission and make his presence known to the host family.

No matter the pressure, a member must not divulge to any one the inner workings of the family. Whether it is to the police, a civilian or a member of another family, the secrets must be kept. Sometimes, even if a member is wrongly imprisoned for a crime of another member, he is obligated not to reveal the truth.

Finally, when a crime has been committed to a member's own person or family, he must not go to the authority and seek resolution. Instead, he must take matters into his own hands or have the offending member pay for his crimes. If the victim is unable to do so, he must seek the help of those within the family.

Omerta is the main reason why mafia crimes are difficult to solve in open court. This is because of the layers upon layers of secrets, the code of silence and the extreme sense of loyalty even to rival families.

1910s reflected the beginning of the Prohibition. It was a nationwide ban on alcohol, including its importation, production, transportation, and sale and even in some states consumption. Chicago then was a place of riots and fighting among street gangs. When the Prohibition was implemented, Big Jim Colosimo, an owner of several brothels, seized control of the gangs and made a lucrative business out of smuggling alcohol. Due to the demand, profit flowed and it became necessary for Colosimo to expand his organization. Criminal activities in the area included bribery, prostitution, fencing, money laundering, gambling, extortion, racketeering, gun running and other activities.

To support the growth of his growing empire, Colosimo brought in Johnny Torrio as his picciotto or enforcer. Torrio in turn needed additional muscle to look after Colosimo's brothels and among his new hires is a 20-year old small time gangster from New York, named Al Capone.

Chapter 2 – Birth of Scarface- His Early Years

"Do not mistake my kindness for weakness. I am kind to everyone, but if you are unkind to me, it will not be weakness that you will remember me for."

-Al Capone

On January 17, 1899, Gabriele Capone and his wife Teresina Raiola gave birth to Alphonse Gabriel Capone in Brooklyn, New York. To reflect his American citizenship, he was called by his American name, Al. The couple immigrated to the United States from Italy. Gabriel was a barber from Naples and Teresina was a seamstress from Salerno. With his parents and eight other siblings, Capone lived in the slums at 95 Navy Street and later in 38 Garfield Place in Park Slope Brooklyn.

During his childhood, Capone was surrounded by a diverse culture of other immigrants, from Ireland, Germany, Sweden and China. Due to the impoverished situation faced by most immigrants starting in a foreign country, Al was also surrounded by harsh people who brawled and fought over already minimal resources.

Although he was considered a bright and promising student in his Catholic school, Capone was always in trouble in school. He was finally expelled when he hit a teacher in the face. From then starting at age 14, he worked several odds jobs, from selling at a candy store to arranging pins in a bowling alley. It is during these times where Capone, while working on a club a few blocks away from his house, is said to have found his mentor, Johnny Torrio.

Torrio was a small but charismatic businessman. He became a sort of champion to fellow Italians and Capone was enthralled by this person. Torrio employed Capone by giving him pocket money for running errands. As their mentoring relationship developed, Torrio began to trust Capone more and more. Capone on the other hand witnessed the life of a successful and wealthy businessman, who was respected by all. Despite the illegalities of Torrio's source of wealth, Capone learned from Torrio the value of an outward decent life that is funded by a secret and dark life.

As a tough teenager, Capone became a member of several gangs, South Brooklyn Rippers, the Forty Thieves Juniors and the Five Point Juniors. These gangs gave Capone the freedom he was desperately looking for and the avenue to express his youthful energies. Another need of Capone that was satisfied by the gangs and Torrio was that of wealth. As an immigrant, the goal was to acquire wealth in the United States as the land of opportunity and this was Capone's goal too.

Torrio referred Capone to an owner of the Coney Island bar Harvard Inn, who employed Capone as bartender and as a bouncer. During one of the regular nights, Capone made an indecent remark to a woman, "Honey, you have a nice ass and I mean that as a compliment." The woman's brother punched Capone and used a knife to slash Capone three times across the face. From those three scars of the knife wound, Capone earned the nickname he hated, Scarface.

At age 19, Capone met his future wife, Mary "Mae" Coughlin. An Irish immigrant who was two years older, she was from a middle class family. On 1918, Mae gave birth to Capone's first son, Albert Francis Capone, the parents later married. Torrio was the godfather. With a family, Capone worked as bookkeeper and seems to have left his dark past. However, the death of his father from a heart disease, prompted Capone to resume his relationship with Torrio. At age 20, Capone was invited by his mentor to move to Chicago. Capone was more than willing.

Chapter 3 – Path to Ascension- Career in Chicago

"It's all yours, Al."

-Johnny Torrio

Earning from his income as a bouncer, Capone purchased an unassuming house in 7244 South Prairie Avenue. Although his mentor was Torrio, his boss was Colosimo the owner of the brothels. Colosimo exposed Capone to a life of luxury, wearing tailored coats, diamond-studded jewelry and parties with high society.

Colosimo on May of 1920 was called by Torrio to inspect a delivery arriving at one of Chicago's cafes. Upon his arrival, Colosimo was shot and killed. Allegedly, Torrio ordered the hit since he is in line to inherit the business. Further allegations link Capone as the hit man.

With Torrio inheriting the business and Capone as the new right hand man, Capone suddenly found himself to be the second in command of Chicago's largest organized crime group with millions of dollars in revenue per year. With the Prohibition in full swing, demand for alcohol increased and the need for more venues to sell them like the bars and brothels also increased. Business was booming and Capone was just one position below the top of it.

He was elevated from this position by Torrio because he was able to use all his past experiences in improving the business. From his early childhood as a member of gangs, he becomes brusque, assertive and almost domineering. From his previous employment as a bookkeeper, he was able to create more efficient systems and processes in the handling of funds and generating profit. From his start as a bouncer, he rose up the ranks as managing the headquarters of the business itself.

Despite his successes, Capone maintained an ideal and respectable façade. He moved his mother and siblings from New York to his Chicago house with his wife and son. To maintain his standing in the community, he pretended to be a seller of used furniture. The deeper his sins in his business became, the more he lavished his family by turning them into the ideal American family.

Such was the trust between Capone and Torrio that when Torrio went to Italy to bring his aging mother to their birthplace, Capone was left in charge. Capone surrounded himself with people, whom he can trust in the absence of Torrio. He employed his brothers, Frank as liaison to the government officials he paid off and Ralph as manager to newly opened businesses. With his own family in place in the business, Capone focused on the gambling joints and racing tracks of Torrio's growing empire. However, this decision of including his family in the business will haunt Capone forever.

During an election of new officials, Capone tried to ensure the victory of the politicians under his payroll. He kidnapped the election workers and threatened the voters themselves. To regain control of the city, more than seventy cops were dispersed and went undercover wearing civilian clothes. During the cops' rounds, Capone's brother, Frank was walking the streets and was recognized by the police. Unprepared, possibly because of their undercover attire, Frank was shot with several bullets and was killed.

Capone retaliated; he ordered the kidnapping and murder of officials, stole ballot boxes and won the government positions for his politicians. Capone ordered an opulent funeral for his brother but instead of calm and mourning, he had to restrain himself from declaring war against the police when the same cops who shot his brother were ordered to observe the funeral.

With Capone at his side, Torrio gained more control over Chicago. Millions were being profited from their various activities and it became necessary for them to expand to other territories. However, these other areas were controlled by another mafia. Tension arose as boundaries were blurred and disputes on claims were being issued. Torrio because he was cheated on a deal by the head of the rival group, lost his patience and ordered a hit. War broke between the two groups and Torrio had to escape away from Chicago. For a while, Torrio was safe but his enemies found him. He was shot in the abdomen, legs, groin, lungs and jaw. He was repeatedly hit with a Billy club because the assassins ran out of bullets for the shot in Torrio's skull. Torrio survived. In respect of his vows towards Omerta, Torrio never named his would-be murderers but he was forever changed. In 1925, he said to the 26 year old Capone, "It's all yours, Al."

Chapter 4 – Height of Power- the Boss

"Do I do business with Canadian racketeers? I don't even know what street Canada is on."

-Al Capone

As the capo crimine, Don Capone was protected by his politicians, ran networks that reached Canada, controlled gambling houses, brothels, nightclubs, distilleries and breweries and even in legitimate businesses. He held Chicago firmly in his grips and earned another nickname, "The Big Fellow." He was a force to be reckoned with; people both loved and feared him. He was now not only wealthy but also powerful and influential. He became a unique and new kind of mafia boss, he was a celebrity. Capone's group, the Chicago Outfit became one of the most successful and dangerous in the entire country.

Violence became more rampant under Capone's leadership but it was all under his permission. Gun battles, executions, beatings and bombings were occurring. Civilians were spared but competitors, rivals and the authorities were intimidated. As his soldatos rose in number, independent gangs dwindled. Capone became a sort of lord of Chicago. He defied Prohibition by manufacturing, transporting and selling alcohol. With the profits, he opened more businesses that were free from any intrusions from the government.

Whether it was a way to soothe his guilty conscience or a genuine care for the poor, Capone used his money to open soup kitchens. He fed people, ordered storeowners to give clothes and food to the poor and the bills were charged to Capone. The public saw him as a Robin Hood figure, Capone received public sympathy. He was said to have provided milk rations to school children. When someone is injured during his soldatos fights, he would pay for the hospital bills. He would buy entire boxes in operas and circuses and give the seats to the poor.

Behind the facade, he was a cold-blooded killer. Though there is no document that can prove the number of people killed, it was thought that Capone was personally responsible for the death of at least 12 people. Hundreds could have also been killed under Capone's orders. Anyone who defied Capone was executed.

Capone also knew that although the public loved him, those who belonged in his world were envious and hated him. He also walked the streets unarmed but he always had at least two bodyguards on his side. He traveled by car and sat at the back seat with one person on either side. He only moved in the night and only risked the day when it was really needed. During critical nights, train stations were surprised to Capone and a small group renting an entire train car. They would ride throughout the night.

On the rare events that the police could have arrested Capone, the code of Omerta protected him from any incrimination. He also had an alibi or a witness that turned a blind eye for Capone.

Chapter 5 – Life of Luxury- His Home, Preferences & Lifestyle

"Public service is my motto. Ninety percent of the people in Chicago drink and gamble. I've tried to serve them decent liquor and square games."

-Al Capone

Capone having reached his goal of wealth, he indulged himself in all manners of luxuries. He bought a 14 room sprawling estate in Palm Island. It has a waterfront pool, a small casino, a small harbor for his yacht and a magnificent view of the lake. With over $60- $100 million in annual revenues just from selling illegal liquor alone, he had plenty of money to spare. He will often walk the streets while holding rolls of bills. He became a patron of jazz music and invited the best musicians across the country. Instead of a fortified base of operations, his headquarters were a nine room suite at the Metropole Hotel.

His favorite nickname was not Scarface, Big Fella or Boss but Snorky. This word means fashionable and elegant. Capone relished on the attention of people who flattered and complimented him on his looks, style and unique sense of fashion. He ordered custom made and colorful suits, expensive cigars, gourmet food and costly jewelry. He wore a white fedora hat and showed off his famous 11.5 carat diamond pinky ring.

His net worth is estimated to be more than $1 billion, although analysts say this figure could be an exaggeration. Local Michigan legend says that Capone hid and buried money everywhere, especially in the street now called Million Dollar Road. However, it is important to note that whatever money and wealth amassed by Capone, it belongs to the mafia as a group and not to one individual, even the boss.

Chapter 6 – Friends & Foes- His Allies & Enemies

"I have built my organization upon fear."

-Al Capone

Capone knew the value of friends outside the organization. Due to his childhood experiences, he was open to developing relationships outside his fellow Italians. He surrounded himself with powerful allies, who occupied the highest seats in Chicago. Future Mayor William Thompson promised to reopen illegal saloons; his declaration prompted the support of Capone with $250,000 in campaign contribution. Bulwarks of Thompson's political rival were bombed by Capone.

Newspaper editor Harry Read was also befriended by Capone. Aside from protecting Capone, Read advised him in public relations concerns. Read told him to make himself visible since hiding can only signal guilt. Capone took his advice and he regularly attended operas, sports and even charitable events. This behavior of living in the public eye was almost unheard of in the secretive lives of a capo crimine. It worked to Capone's advantage, for a while he was well-loved by Chicago citizens, adding another layer of protection from law enforcement.

As powerful as Capone had become, there were still others who chose to defy him. Dion O' Banion had his own alcohol smuggling business along with a chain of flower shops. He was a very courteous, happy and pleasant person to deal with, who always offered his hand to shake people he met. This he does while having the other hand in his gun pocket. After cheating Capone on a deal, Banion bragged about it. While Banion was arranging flowers, three gunmen arrived and shot him. Though unconfirmed, it was said that it was Capone's men. The leadership vacuum left by Banion's death was conveniently filled by Capone.

Perhaps the worst enemy of Capone could have been another capo crimine, Hymie Weiss. A Polish immigrant, Weiss inherited the position left by Banion and one of his standing orders was the death of Capone. He was able to stage two unsuccessful attacks on Capone, one while Capone was inside a car and the other while in a bar. Capone survived every time, always due to the protection of Capone's loyal bodyguards. Fed up with the repeated attempts, weeks after the last attempt, Weiss himself was assassinated. No one took credit for the hit but it was widely believed to be under the orders of Capone.

Chapter 7 – Hits & Misses- Modus Operandi, Massacres & Failed Assassinations

"You can get much farther with a kind word and a gun that you can with a kind word alone."

-Al Capone

There were two massacres associated with Capone; the most famous is the St. Valentines' and the less known Adonis Club. Capone's old rival, the North Side Gang, was targeted to gain more control of the business in Chicago.

Capone was ruthless in his tactics; he had his men rent an apartment across the warehouse where his targets were working. On the morning of attack, February 14, 1929, he ordered his men to wear police clothes and act as if they were raiding the warehouse. Shocked, the targets only obeyed when they were asked to line up along a wall and did not even struggle. Using machine and shot guns, all were executed. Although one of victims was conscious for three hours after the attack, the police did not get any information on the attackers. He refused to identify his own killers, honoring Omerta.

The Adonis Club Massacre occurred when Capone was due to give a Christmas Day party. However, Capone received a tip that some of his rivals will be crashing the party. Instead of canceling, Capone chose to push forward. The rivals came and were loud and insulting. After they have eaten and drank to their hearts content, the gatecrashers were personally entertained by Capone, using a baseball bat. The rivals were shot and dumped outside town.

Capone himself narrowly survived an assassination attempt. Banion, the florist, had loyal men who planned to avenge his death. While eating at a restaurant, ten cars moved past the place where Capone was and fired machine guns and shotguns. Capone's bodyguard threw him on the ground and lay on top of him for the duration of the attack. Capone was unharmed. While in transport, unknown assassins tried to kill him but only managed to damage his car.

However, Capone chose to take matter of his security seriously. He outfitted his cars with bullet-proof glass and thicker doors and frames. He bought hideouts scattered outside Chicago. Tunnels were dug to provide him escape routes in case of emergencies.

Chapter 8 – Fall from Grace- Trials, Imprisonment & Release

"When I sell liquor, it's bootlegging. When my patrons serve it on a silver tray on Lakeshore Drive, it's hospitality."

-Al Capone

Capone was arrested and also imprisoned for several times. However because of Omerta, police always ad to release him after only spending a few hours up to one night in previous since there was just insufficient evidence. The unknowing masses of Chicago lost their faith in Capone because of the violence of his family. Out of the 28 worst criminals listed in Chicago then, Capone was number one. Then President Hoover himself ordered to find a way to arrest of Capone.

Ironically, Capone was truly convicted not because of the illegal activities he ran or the murders he ordered but something more anticlimactic, tax evasion. During his time, there was a vague area in taxation laws that assumed illegal gambling earnings as non-taxable. However, a previous ruling made it clear that not only was it taxable but also it had to be reported. Law enforcement found a chink in Capone's impervious armor and multi-layered defenses. Capone, who never filed an income tax return, with various fronts and middlemen that were used as dummies for Capone's own properties, was filed tax evasion charges.

A trial was held and he was ordered to pay more than $200,000 in back taxes. He was also accused of violating Prohibition rules. He pleaded guilty hoping that he will be allowed to plea bargain. He was refused and he tried to change his plea to not guilty. He was again refused and Capone attempted to bribe the jury. The jury was replaced at the last minute before the trial. Out of the 23 counts of the various charges, Capone was found guilty of only 5. Still, he was sentenced to 10 years imprisonment in a federal prison and 1 year in a county jail.

Immediately upon his incarceration, Capone took control of his situation. His cell was furnished with mirrors, rugs, furnishings and other lavish decorations. News of his privileged life in prison, he was moved to Alcatraz. There, Capone had no connections; he neither had influence nor friends. For the first time, he played by the rules and became an ideal prisoner.

Weighing 250 lbs, Capone was suffering from syphilis and gonorrhea. He was also withdrawing from his drug addiction. He spent his days in prison making shoes. During the eleventh and last year of his sentence, he spent the remainder of his days in the prison hospital because of the effects of neurosyphilis.

He was released on parole on 1939.

Chapter 9 – Vacant Throne- Later Years, Death & the Aftermath

"Be careful who you call your friends. I'd rather have four quarters than one hundred pennies."

-Al Capone

After his release, Capone was confined to the hospital. Due to a complication of syphilis when he was still young, he developed paresis. He was supposed to be admitted in Johns Hopkins but the hospital refused him because of his reputation. Union Memorial took him instead and in gratitude, Capone donated two weeping cherry trees. Capone chose to leave the hospital on 1940.

Due to his paresis that caused neurological paralysis which manifested in mental deterioration, loss of memory functions and a wide range of delusions and mood swings, Capone was assessed with having the mental capability of a 12 year old child. Unable to reassume control of the Mob, he retired.

At his mansion in Florida, Capone had a stroke; he survived but later contracted pneumonia. On January 25, 1947 at 48 years old, Capone suffered a fatal heart attack.

To accommodate his massive bulk a large $2000 bronze casket was used. He wore a dark blue suit, silk socks and the classic black and white gangster shoes. Thousands of dollars worth of wreaths, baskets and arrangements arrived with even a 7 foot cross entirely made of flowers. He was buried at Mount Carmel Cemetery in Illinois, beside his father and brother.

The New York Times headline read, "End of an Evil Dream," at the time of Capone's death. However, the headline was only partially true, it was indeed the end of Capone dreaming but the dream persisted. Capone's family continued the

Immediately upon his incarceration, Capone took control of his situation. His cell was furnished with mirrors, rugs, furnishings and other lavish decorations. News of his privileged life in prison, he was moved to Alcatraz. There, Capone had no connections; he neither had influence nor friends. For the first time, he played by the rules and became an ideal prisoner.

Weighing 250 lbs, Capone was suffering from syphilis and gonorrhea. He was also withdrawing from his drug addiction. He spent his days in prison making shoes. During the eleventh and last year of his sentence, he spent the remainder of his days in the prison hospital because of the effects of neurosyphilis.

He was released on parole on 1939.

Chapter 9 – Vacant Throne- Later Years, Death & the Aftermath

"Be careful who you call your friends. I'd rather have four quarters than one hundred pennies."

-Al Capone

After his release, Capone was confined to the hospital. Due to a complication of syphilis when he was still young, he developed paresis. He was supposed to be admitted in Johns Hopkins but the hospital refused him because of his reputation. Union Memorial took him instead and in gratitude, Capone donated two weeping cherry trees. Capone chose to leave the hospital on 1940.

Due to his paresis that caused neurological paralysis which manifested in mental deterioration, loss of memory functions and a wide range of delusions and mood swings, Capone was assessed with having the mental capability of a 12 year old child. Unable to reassume control of the Mob, he retired.

At his mansion in Florida, Capone had a stroke; he survived but later contracted pneumonia. On January 25, 1947 at 48 years old, Capone suffered a fatal heart attack.

To accommodate his massive bulk a large $2000 bronze casket was used. He wore a dark blue suit, silk socks and the classic black and white gangster shoes. Thousands of dollars worth of wreaths, baskets and arrangements arrived with even a 7 foot cross entirely made of flowers. He was buried at Mount Carmel Cemetery in Illinois, beside his father and brother.

The New York Times headline read, "End of an Evil Dream," at the time of Capone's death. However, the headline was only partially true, it was indeed the end of Capone dreaming but the dream persisted. Capone's family continued the business but in a more low profile but equally effective management. So secretive was Capone's outfit that it is still unknown who inherited the leadership.

Allegedly, Capone chose Frank Nitti, one of his enforcers, as his successor. However, it was widely believed that Nitti's underboss, Paul Ricca was the real boss. Under Nitti or Ricca's leadership, Capone's legacy outside Chicago, reaching even Hollywood where it entrenched itself in labor unions.

In the next 10 years, law enforcement was able to deal a significant blow on the organization with various raids under the leadership of determined politicians. Fast forward to the 20th century, the Department of Justice launched Operation Family Secrets; its objective was to indict several members of the organization.

As of today, from Capone's thousands of associates, soldatos and caporegimes, the Outfit is now estimated to have only 28 members headed by an 86 year old John DiFronzo.

Whether the attention seeking Capone will approve or not, Capone's distant relatives are stars to a reality TV show. His great nephew, Dominic is the boss of the show, The Capones. It is about the family running a pizza business.

Conclusion

No one can deny the contradictions of Al Capone's character; he was charismatic but ruthless, greedy but charitable, warm to friends but cold-blooded to his enemies. He was a devout Catholic and family man but he opened brothels and prostitution dens. He is calm and controlled but his temper led him to personally commit murders.

He truly turned the American dream into reality, albeit a dark and sinister version of it. From a poor childhood life living in the slums, he worked as a minor errand boy, a bouncer, a bookkeeper, all the way to becoming a petty soldato to a capo crimine. At the height of his power, he was considered the capo de tutti cappi, the boss of all bosses in all but name.

From tattered clothes to diamond rings, from a small house to a sprawling estate, from serving to leading the mafia, his unstoppable rise can only be matched by his meteoric decline. He was convicted because of a minor charge, he was reduced to doing menial tasks in prison and a debilitating disease weakened his once commanding mental faculties.

Al Capone's legacy endures today, be it in the form of the Outfit that still exists or the legend that continues to pique the curiosity and interest of people around the world.

Thank you

Thank you very much for taking part in this book. If you enjoyed this book, please, leave a review on Amazon. It would be greatly appreciated! Your review will help other people recognize value that this book provides.

This book is the beginning of a series that are about the lives of other legendary US gangsters. Look for other biographies of Capone's peers at www.garynites.com.

Thank you so much for being with me.

Printed in Dunstable, United Kingdom